W9-BDA-935

PIERRE BERTON

The Battles of the War of · 1812 ·

CANADA UNDER SIEGE

ILLUSTRATIONS BY HENRY VAN DER LINDE

M&S

An M&S Paperback Original from
McClelland & Stewart Inc.
The Canadian Publishers

An M&S Paperback Original from McClelland & Stewart Inc.

First printing September 1991

Copyright © 1991 by Pierre Berton Enterprises Ltd.

Canadian Cataloguing in Publication Data

Berton, Pierre, 1920–
  Canada under siege

(Adventures in Canadian history. The battles of
the War of 1812)
"An M&S paperback original".
Includes index.
ISBN 0-7710-1431-7

1. Canada – History – War of 1812 – Campaigns –
Juvenile literature.* I. Van der Linde, Henry.
II. Title. III. Series: Berton, Pierre, 1920–
Adventures in Canadian history. The battles of
the War of 1812.

FC442.B47 1991   j971.03′4   C91-094454-7
E359.85.B47 1991

Cover design by Tania Craan
Text design by Martin Gould
Cover illustration by Scott Cameron
Interior illustrations by Henry Van Der Linde
Maps by James Loates
Editor: Peter Carver

Typesetting by Pickwick
Printed and bound in Canada

McClelland & Stewart Inc.
The Canadian Publishers
481 University Avenue
Toronto, Ontario
M5G 2E9

CONTENTS

Maps appear on pages 24–5 and 70

Adventures in Canadian History

CANADA UNDER SIEGE

Private in the 49th Regiment of Foot, garrisoned at York, 1812

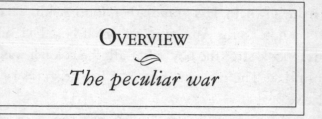

Overview

The peculiar war

WHEN WAR BROKE out between the United States and Canada in June of 1812, John Richardson rushed to join the colours. He was only fifteen – a slight, curly-headed, clean shaven youth – but, unlike so many of his neighbours, he was eager to serve his country.

Many of his neighbours on the Detroit river were recent arrivals from the United States, reluctant to fight their former compatriots. But Richardson came of solid Canadian stock. His mother's father, John Askin, was a famous fur trader. His grandmother was an Ottawa Indian of the Algonquin nation. And so young John, to his considerable delight, found himself accepted as a "gentleman volunteer" in a regular regiment – the British 41st – stationed in Fort Amherstburg not far from the present site of Windsor. In the next thirty months, he probably saw more of the War of 1812 than any other teenager in Upper Canada.

After fifteen months of fighting, Richardson was captured by the Americans – a capture that tells us a good deal about that most peculiar of wars. Unlike so many prisoners in so many jail cells around the world, he could be fairly sure of decent treatment by his enemies, because he knew so many of them. His grandfather, John Askin, had only to write a note to the American colonel at Fort Detroit asking him to look after the boy. After all, the colonel was Askin's son-in-law. The man in charge of his prison was another relative.

The War of 1812, then, must be seen as a civil war fought by men and women on both sides of a border that all had ignored until hostilities broke out. Many were former neighbours who spoke the same language and were often related to one another. Unlike the Richardsons, three out of every five were former Americans.

Some had come up from the United States after the American Revolution. These "Tories", as their compatriots called them, were fiercely loyal to the British Crown. Canadians know them as "United Empire Loyalists." They formed the backbone of the volunteer civilian army, known as the militia.

The others were more recent arrivals. They came to Canada because the land was cheap and taxes almost non-existent. They wanted to be left alone to clear the land of stumps, to drain the marshes, till the soil, and harvest their crops of wheat, barley and corn, or tend the apple, pear and cherry trees that grew so abundantly along the border.

For them, life was hard enough without war. They built their own cabins and barns with the help of their neighbours and, since there was scarcely anything resembling a shop or a store, they made everything themselves, from farm implements to the homespun clothing that was the universal dress. Those villages that existed at all were mere huddles of shacks. Communication was difficult and sometimes impossible. Newspapers were virtually unknown. In the single room schoolhouses, children learned to read, write, and figure – not much more.

These people didn't want to fight any more than their counterparts, the civilian soldiers south of the border. It was indeed a peculiar war that moved along in fits and starts, like a springless buggy bumping over a dirt track. At harvest time and seeding, farmers on both sides deserted or were sent off to tend to their crops. In winter, nothing moved; it was too cold to fight, and so each autumn all activity was postponed until spring.

It was, like so many conflicts, a very silly war. Communication was so bad that hundreds of soldiers, not to mention generals, had no idea it had begun. The last bloody battle was fought long after peace had been declared. The problems that had caused the war in the first place – Great Britain's attacks on American shipping – were solved well before the war ended. But the war went on – men were maimed and killed, farms were vandalized, barns were burned, whole communities put to the torch, and "traitors" hanged for no purpose.

Why were young Canadians like John Richardson fighting young Americans along the international border? The Canadians who fought did so to protect their country from attack. The Americans were fighting for something less tangible – their honour. Once again, they felt, the British were pushing them around. The War of 1812 was in many ways a continuation of the War of Independence fought forty years before.

It started with Napoleon Bonaparte, the dictator of France. Bonaparte wanted to conquer all of Europe, and so the British found themselves locked in a long and bloody struggle with him – a struggle that began with the great British naval victory at Trafalgar and ended a decade later with the famous battle of Waterloo.

But in their zeal to conquer Napoleon, the British pushed the Americans too far. By boarding American ships on the high seas and kidnapping American sailors for service in the Royal Navy – on the grounds that these seamen were actually British deserters – they got the Americans' backs up. Then, in order to strangle the French by a sea blockade, the British announced they would seize any ship that dared sail directly for a French port. By 1812, they had captured four hundred American vessels, some within sight of the U.S. coast.

That was too much. The United States at last declared war on Great Britain. Since it couldn't attack England directly, it determined to give the British a bloody nose by invading its colony, Canada.

To former President Thomas Jefferson, that seemed "a mere matter of marching." Surely the United States, with a population of eight million, could easily defeat a mere three hundred thousand Canadians!

The odds, however, weren't quite as unequal as Jefferson supposed. Great Britain had 17,000 regular troops stationed in Upper and Lower Canada. The entire U.S. regular army numbered only 7,000, many of them badly trained.

Moreover, the British controlled the water routes – Lakes Huron, Erie and Ontario, and also the St. Lawrence River. For that was the key to both mobility and communication. The roads were almost worthless when they existed at all – not much more than rutted cart tracks. Everything – supplies, troops and weapons – moved by water.

When the war broke out, the Americans were prevented from using this water highway by the presence of the Royal Navy on the lakes. A British express canoe could move swiftly and fearlessly all the way to Lake Superior, carrying dispatches. But the American high command had difficulty communicating at all, which explains why its outposts didn't know for a month that the war was on. The Americans had to use express riders – bold men on horseback, plunging through a jungle of forest and swamp and exposed at every turn to an Indian ambush.

No wonder, then, that almost from the outset the War of 1812 developed into a shipbuilding contest, with both sides feverishly hammering men-of-war to completion in a race to control the lakes.

The Indians were another asset for the British. The

Americans had turned them into enemies, burning their crops and villages and hunting them down like wild animals. In American eyes, the Indians were an obstruction to be pushed aside or eliminated as the pioneers and settlers moved resolutely westward. But the Canadians hadn't fought the Indians since the days of the French-English wars fifty years before. They saw them as harvesters of fur, or, as in the case of the Mohawks of the Grand Valley, loyal subjects of the King.

The American attitude caused John Richardson's boyhood friend, Tecumseh, to move into Upper Canada from the U.S. with his followers to fight on the British side. The native allies numbered no more than 2,000 in all, but with their woodcraft they made a formidable enemy. The Americans were terrified of the Indians. The mere hint that a force of natives was advancing could send a chill through the blood of the citizen soldiers of Ohio or Kentucky.

As a member of the regular army, John Richardson wore a scarlet uniform and carried a musket almost as tall as himself. This awkward, muzzle-loading "Brown Bess" was the basic infantry weapon – and a notoriously inaccurate one. The little one-ounce (.03 kg) ball, wobbling down the smooth barrel, could fly off in any direction. Richardson and his fellow soldiers didn't bother to aim their weapons; they pointed them in the direction of the enemy, waited for the command, and then fired in unison.

The effect of several hundred men, marching in line and in step, shoulders touching, and advancing behind a spray of lead, could be devastating. The noise alone was terrifying. The musket's roar makes the crack of a modern rifle sound like a popgun. Smokeless powder was unknown; after the first volley the battlefield was shrouded in a thick fog of grey.

It required twelve separate movements to load and fire a musket. A well-drilled soldier could get off two or three shots a minute. By that time he was usually close enough to the enemy to rely on his bayonet.

Young Richardson learned to remove a paper cartridge from his pouch, tear off the top with his teeth, pour a little powder in the firing pan and the rest down the barrel. Then he stuffed it with wadding, tapped it tight with his ramrod and dropped in the ball. When he pulled the trigger it engaged the flintlock whose spark (he hoped) would ignite the powder in the pan and send a flash through a pinhole, exploding the charge in the barrel. As Richardson himself discovered at the Battle of Frenchtown later that year, it didn't always work. The phrase "a flash in the pan" comes down to us from those days.

Some of the American woodsmen used the famous Tennessee rifle, a far more accurate weapon because of the spiral groove inside the barrel. That put a spin on the ball – in the same way a pitcher does in baseball – making it far easier to hit the target. However, it was slower to load and was used mainly by snipers or individual soldiers.

A more terrible weapon was the cannon, which operated on the same flintlock principle as the musket. From the

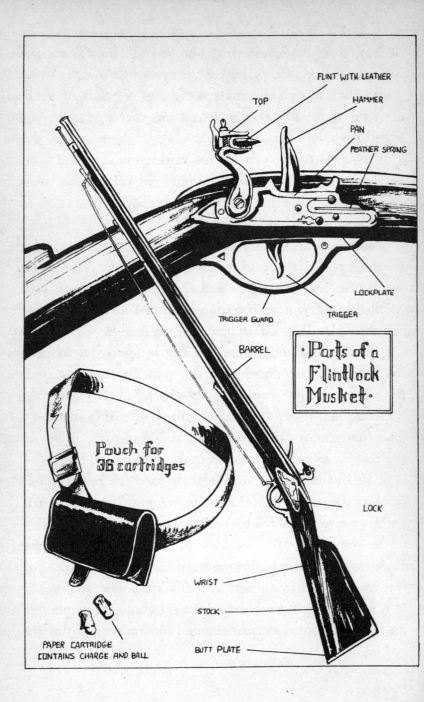

FLINT WITH LEATHER

TOP

HAMMER

PAN

FEATHER SPRING

LOCKPLATE

TRIGGER GUARD

TRIGGER

BARREL

· Parts of a Flintlock Musket ·

Pouch for 36 cartridges

LOCK

WRIST

STOCK

BUTT PLATE

PAPER CARTRIDGE
CONTAINS CHARGE AND BALL

tiny three-pounders (1.4 kg) to the big twenty-four-pounders (11 kg), these weapons were identified by the weight of shot they hurled at the ramparts of the defenders. A sixteen-pound (7 kg) ball of solid pig iron (known as "roundshot") could knock down a file of two dozen men. Bombs – hollowed out shot, crammed with powder and bric-à-brac, and fused to explode in mid-air – were even more devastating. Every soldier feared the canister and grape shot – sacks or metal canisters filled with musket balls that broke apart in the air, sending scores of projectiles whirling above the enemy.

Crude as they seem to us now, these weapons caused a dreadful havoc for the soldiers who fought in the war. Men with mangled limbs and jagged wounds faced searing pain because anaesthetics had not been invented. Yet, grievously wounded men pleaded with army surgeons to amputate a wounded limb as quickly as possible for fear of gangrene. They swallowed a tot of rum or whisky, held a bullet ("biting the bullet") between their gritted teeth, and endured fearful agony as the knives and saws did their work.

Sanitation in the field was primitive, for science had not yet discovered that diseases were caused by germs. Measles, typhus, typhoid, influenza, and dysentery probably put more men out of action than the enemy. The universal remedy was liquor – a daily glass of strong Jamaica rum for the British, a quarter pint (0.2 L) of raw whisky for the Americans. In battle after battle, the combatants on both sides were at least half drunk. Hundreds of youths who had never touched hard liquor in their lives learned to stiffen their resolve through alcohol in the War of 1812.

These were civilian soldiers, members of the militia. In Canada, the Sedentary Militia, largely untrained, was available in times of crisis. Every fit male between 18 and 60 was required to serve in it when needed. Few had uniforms, and those who did were as tattered as beggars. Often they were sent home to their farms after a battle to be called up later.

Some signed up in the Incorporated Militia of Upper Canada for the duration of the war. These were young men inspired by patriotism, a sense of adventure, or the bounty of 80 dollars paid to every volunteer upon enlistment. In Lower Canada, a similar body of the Select Embodied Militia, composed of men between 18 and 25, was drawn by lot to serve for a minimum of two years. They were paid and trained as regular soldiers. In addition some regular units were also recruited in Canada, bearing such names as The Glengarry Fencibles or the Canadian Voltigeurs.

The American draftees and volunteers were engaged by the various states for shorter periods – as little as a month, as much as a year. Most refused to serve beyond that period; few were properly trained. Born of revolution and dedicated to absolute democracy, the United States had decided against a large standing army. The citizen soldiers even elected their own officers – an awkward and not very efficient process, sneered at by the regulars. And they were recruited to fight *only* in defence of their country.

That caused a major problem for the United States. Legally, the state militia didn't have to cross the border. Hundreds who had been drafted reluctantly used that excuse when their superiors tried to goad them into attacking Canada. Jefferson had said it was "a mere matter of marching," but when the armies reached the border, the marching stopped.

They didn't want to fight any more than their former compatriots, now tilling the fields and tending the orchards on the other side. That was one of the reasons why this peculiar war ended in stalemate. The Americans derived very little benefit from it; nor did the Indians, who were eventually betrayed by both sides when the peace talks were held. The only real victors were the Canadians, who got no territory but gained something less tangible, yet in the end more precious. Having helped to hurl back five American armies, the plain people who had once been so indifferent to the war developed both a sense of pride and a sense of community. They had come through the fire and they had survived. In a very real sense the War of 1812 marked the first faint stirrings of a united Canadian nation.

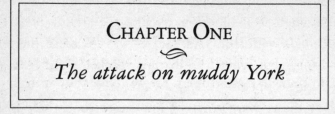

CHAPTER ONE

The attack on muddy York

THERE WAS A TIME, when Canada was young – and still a colony of Great Britain – when an invading army from a foreign land crossed her borders, intent on conquest. There was a time when the city of Toronto – then a small, muddy village of no more than a thousand souls, known as York – was attacked and captured by American forces. There was a time when the settled communities of Ontario – then known as Upper Canada – were robbed and burned by men who spoke the same language and sprang from the same roots as Canadians.

The time was 1813. The month was April, when the first buds were sprouting on the chokecherries that lined the concession roads and the first robins were warbling in the cedar forests along the Humber and Don rivers. On the morning of the 26th, those residents of York who had risen early were faced with a dismaying spectacle. On Lake Ontario an American fleet, bristling with cannon, lay just off the mouth of the Don.

The war with the United States, which we call the War of 1812, was almost a year old. Twice the previous summer the Americans had tried to invade Canada – once from Amherstburg directly across from Fort Detroit, and again at Queenston on the Niagara river. Twice they had been hurled back, with Detroit and Michigan territory seized by British, Canadian and Indian forces. Now they were trying again, with a new army crammed aboard fourteen ships determined to strike at the capital of Upper Canada.

A shipbuilding contest was underway on Lake Ontario. At the eastern end, at Sackets Harbor, the Americans were frantically trying to add to their fleet. But the British had a big warship of their own under construction at York and another complete. The Americans intended to seize both vessels and add them to their fleet. That would upset the balance of naval power and give them control of the lake.

On the morning of April 26 the Reverend John Strachan, thirty-five years old, a stocky figure in clergyman's black, saw the American fleet through his spyglass. In the events that followed he would play a key role. Strachan had no use for the American settlers who were pouring into the province from the border states, bringing with them – in his view – a godless and materialistic way of life. Strachan believed as strongly in the British colonial system as he did in the Church of England. He was the most energetic man in town: he taught the chosen in his own grammar school, performed weddings, funerals, and christenings, attended military parades, poked his nose regularly into government, and managed to produce a hefty number of books, articles, and pamphlets.

The war had made him tougher. As far he was concerned it was a just war – one that Christians could wage with vigour and a clear conscience.

He was not alone in thinking that way. Aboard the tall ships lurking outside the harbour, bristling with cannon, other men – Americans – equally determined, were preparing for bloody combat. And, as in all wars, their leaders were as certain as John Strachan that *their* cause was just, and that the god of battle stood firmly in their ranks.

The leader of the invasion force was Zebulon Montgomery Pike, the army's newest brigadier-general. At that very moment in his cabin on the American flagship he was scratching out a letter to his wife. Pike knew that it might be his last. "Should I fall," he wrote, "defend my memory and only believe, had I lived, I would have aspired to deeds worthy of your husband."

For most of his military life Pike had yearned to perform deeds of glory that would bring him everlasting fame. But, in spite of a flaming ambition, the laurel had eluded him. He had been a soldier for nineteen of his thirty-four years, but his only action had been an inglorious skirmish on the Canadian border the previous November in which his troops shot at their own men.

He was better known as an explorer than an officer. Pike's Peak, a mountain in the Rockies, bears his name today, even though he didn't discover it, didn't climb it, and didn't come within fifteen miles (25 km) of it.

He was a bold, impulsive man. Serenely confident in his own ability, he felt he was headed for greatness. But promotion had been maddeningly slow. Now, at last, opportunity beckoned. "If we go into Canada," he wrote to a fellow officer, "you will hear of my fame or of my death, for I am determined to seek the Bubble even in the cannon's mouth."

Pike had been chosen to lead the attack on York because his commanding general, Henry Dearborn, was ill, or pretended to be. An indecisive, grotesque pudding of a man, Dearborn was so gross he had to be trundled about in a wheelbarrow. His troops called him "Granny."

The American sailing ships were jammed with fourteen hundred men, six hundred of whom were crowded aboard Pike's flagship *Madison*. As they dropped anchor off what was to become Sunnyside beach, John Strachan, through his spyglass, could see them clambering into the small boats.

The clergyman felt a sense of frustration. Why were there no British or Canadian troops rushing to repel them? The British general, Roger Sheaffe, had a tendency to delay. That maddened Strachan, who saw himself as a military expert.

It is a military axiom that a landing from the water must be halted at the edge of the beach before the enemy can dig in. Because the Americans would have to come ashore in waves, then send the boats back for more troops, Sheaffe's forces would outnumber the invaders in the early stages of the attack. Surely now, Strachan thought, was the time to rush every available man through the woods that separated the garrison from the landing point and hurl the Americans back!

But if Sheaffe faced a dilemma, he didn't show it. Even his critics – and he had many – remarked on his coolness in the events that followed. He was a bulky man, a little ponderous, who hadn't wanted to fight the Americans. The

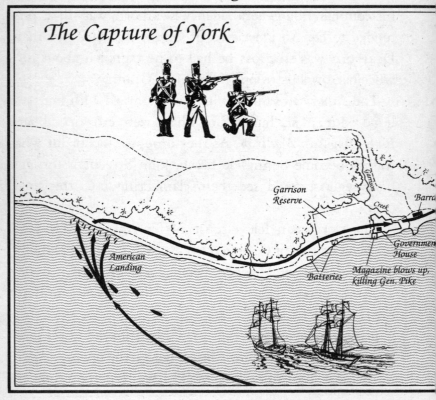

The Capture of York

Garrison Reserve

Garri[son] Creek

Barra[cks]

Government House

American Landing

Batteries

Magazine blows up, killing Gen. Pike

Revolution had split his family, and a sister still lived in Boston. Nonetheless, he was prepared to do his duty.

Alas, he was no gambler. He had waited too long to figure out where the Americans planned to land. Worse, he dispatched his troops piecemeal. He first sent off the Indians to oppose the landing along with a company of Glengarrys. A company of the King's grenadiers followed, and after them, three companies of regulars. And at last, when the militia was finally formed, he sent them under their adjutant-general, Aneas Shaw, to protect the right flank

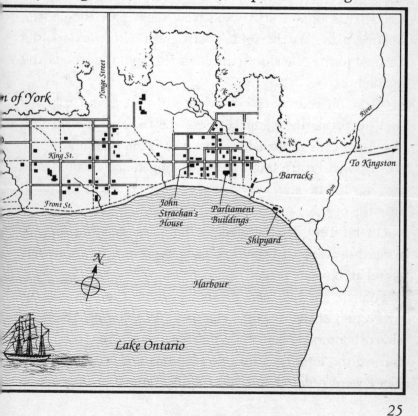

along the Dundas Road. He had two six-pound (2.8 kg) cannon at his disposal, but he didn't believe they could be trundled through the woods and so didn't use them.

At that point things began to go wrong. Shaw got lost. So did the Glengarrys. Not long after the American advance troops were ashore, they were threading their way through the woods, cutting down the disorganized defenders.

Pike himself could not stand being out of the action. From the foredeck of the flagship *Madison*, he could see Captain Benjamin Forsyth's rifle corps pulling for the Canadian shore. A stiff wind blew them past the chosen landing place. As the soldiers struggled with the oars, the painted forms of the Indians emerged from the woods and opened fire.

"Rest on your oars," Forsyth whispered, and told his men to prime their muskets. As the Indians opened fire, the Americans returned it. That was Pike's moment.

"By God! I can't stand here any longer," he shouted, and turning to the staff, cried out, "Jump, come, come, jump into the boat."

Off he went, surrounded by his aides, heading directly toward the centre of the fray, a square, serene figure in blue – and an obvious target.

Forsyth got his men to shore, where they sought the protection of the woods – the natural habitat of American sharpshooters. Pike waded ashore with his men and formed the infantry into two platoons under a high bank. They were ordered to scale the incline and charge across the field with their bayonets. But the British grenadiers poured out of the forest and drove them down the bank back to the water's edge.

The light draught schooners, moving in at close range, sprayed the British with grapeshot, and did terrible damage. The Indians, their morale shattered, vanished from the scene. Caught in a crossfire between the naval guns and the American sharpshooters, the British regulars stumbled back into the woods. They weren't used to this kind of warfare. Their training had been on the broad plains of Europe. And in their scarlet jackets they made easy targets for the American riflemen hidden between logs and trees.

"Show us our enemy, Pike," the British soldiers cried. But they disdained the natural protection of the forest and dropped like grouse at a highland shoot. Of 119 grenadiers, only thirty survived. Two are believed to have fallen through the rotting ice of a deep pond, which is today known as Grenadier Pond.

It didn't occur to them to retreat, any more than it occurred to them to seek cover. At last, unable to dislodge the Americans, their surviving officers led them back toward the Western Battery that guarded the lake road.

By now the din in the woods was deafening – the shouts of the combatants, the war whoops of the Indians, the roar of cannon and musket, and above all this, the piercing notes of Forsyth's bugler trumpeting success.

The naval guns continued to pour a hail of shot into the woods as Pike formed his men into columns and, with a fife and drum corps playing "Yankee Doodle", marched towards York through the woods along the road that hugged the lake.

Ely Playter, a farmer and militia lieutenant, back from scouting the east end of town, turned up just as the first of retreating British staggered out of the woods. Above the sound of music he could hear the cheers of the American sailors as six ships moved up toward the Western Battery. It was here that Sheaffe intended to make a stand. But that would not be easy, for the battery was jammed with men all jostling each other and harassing the gunners.

The six American ships could throw more than two hundred pounds (90 kg) of iron at the battery in a single volley. The twelve British gunners, working largely with old cannon, had scarcely one-third that fire power. And Pike's men had managed to haul two field guns through the woods – a feat that Sheaffe had believed impossible.

But before they could fling themselves at the battery, a dreadful accident occurred. In the cramped quarters, somebody jostled one of the gunners. A spark from a British gunner's slow match fell into a powder magazine. The explosion killed more than a dozen men, scorching others horribly and tearing away the gun platform.

Badly rattled, the regulars tried to remount the big gun. The militia fled. Nobody seemed to know what was to be done. General Sheaffe had left. Outnumbered, he had decided that the town could not be defended. Already he was laying plans to save his regulars and deny the public stores to the enemy.

And so Pike's forces had little opposition as they pushed on along the lake-shore toward Government House and the garrison.

The fleeing militia lost all sense of order. Ely Playter and others tried to rally them without success. Playter realized the garrison was about to be evacuated but did not know that Sheaffe had already decided to pull out and blow up the main magazine on the waterfront below Government House. Within this underground fort were two hundred barrels of gun powder and a vast quantity of cartridge, shells and round shot. Concerned only with saving his regulars, Sheaffe gave little attention to the straggling militia. Several dozen were within a whisper of the magazine.

With the fuses burning, Playter and his men had already been ordered to march off. But the young farmer had left his coat in his quarters. He ran to retrieve it, unaware that the magazine was about to blow.

Pike was within four hundred yards (370 m) of the garrison and ordered his men to hug the ground while he brought up a six-pounder and a howitzer that his men had dragged through the mud and the stumps. He was on the verge of victory and he knew it.

It would be the first American victory after ten months of bitter defeat.

He sat on a stump, waiting for the final attack. One of his

men had captured a Canadian militia sergeant and two of his aides. Pike was about to question them. But at that very instant the ground shook and the world turned dazzling white. An enormous roar split the ears of the attackers as a giant cloud spurted from the blazing magazine to blossom in the sky. From that vast canopy there burst in all directions an eruption of debris – great chunks of masonry, broken beams, gigantic boulders, rocks and stones of every size. This terrifying hail poured down upon the attackers, covering the ground for a thousand feet in every direction, killing or maiming more than a hundred men, striking off arms and legs, crushing chests and beheading bodies.

Ely Playter, who had got his coat back and reached the barrack gate, had an appalling close-up view. Miraculously, he was untouched. He could see the huge boulders dropping all around them, some skipping across the ground, others burying themselves in the mud. He saw men smashed to a pulp.

The British casualties ran to forty, most of them militia. The Americans suffered more than five times that number and the general was among the dying. Zebulon Pike lay helpless among his mangled followers. A huge boulder had crushed his ribs. His aide was dead and so was the unfortunate Canadian sergeant.

Pike's wounds were mortal and he knew it. How humiliating, to be killed by a falling rock! Not for him the gallant death, waving his sword in the teeth of the battle, achieving the instant martyrdom of a Nelson or a Brock. Time only

The main magazine at York blows, sending a terrifying hail of debris in all directions. General Pike, struck by a falling rock, lay helpless among his followers.

for a few gasping phrases for the history books: "Push on, my brave fellows, and avenge your general!"

Unfortunately for the Americans, the British regulars who ought to have surrendered slipped out of the bag before the noose could be pulled tight. The British army escaped to fight another day. And Pike would not go down in history as a military hero, but as one who accidentally gave his name to a mountain that somebody before him had discovered and somebody after him had climbed.

CHAPTER TWO

John Strachan reigns supreme

JOHN STRACHAN, BUSTLING about town seeking the action, hurried back to his house to find his wife in a state of terror. He bundled her and the children off to a friend's home outside the town and then rushed back toward the garrison. He found Sheaffe and the regulars in a ravine getting ready to leave. Strachan later demanded to know why the major-general didn't seize that moment to counterattack, but Sheaffe had no way of knowing of the havoc the explosion had caused among the enemy. The most sensible thing he could do was to burn the naval stores and the big vessel, *Isaac Brock*, under construction in the harbour, and get his men out of town to reinforce Kingston. He was certain that it would be the next target of American attack.

The Americans were furious. The whole object of the expedition had been to capture two British ships. But Sheaffe had burned one and the other had escaped from the harbour before the attack began. Worse, the real army was out of reach – en route to Kingston and safety. Now they had to deal with amateur soldiers and a clergyman – for

Strachan volunteered his services and soon became chief negotiator for the people of York.

Under the terms of the peace treaty, all arms and public stores had to be given to the Americans. The militia were not made prisoners but were paroled – released on the understanding they would no longer take up arms – and thus neutralized for the remainder of the war. Only officers were imprisoned. And private property was to be respected.

There was looting that night, though it was comparatively light. When Mrs. Grant Powell, a prominent society hostess, returned to her home that evening, she found Americans in her house, one of them munching on a piece of loaf sugar. A spirited argument followed with a soldier, a six-footer (1.8 m), getting much the worst of it.

Mrs. Powell told him to go home and mind his own business.

"I wish I could," the soldier replied miserably.

Mrs. Powell relented a little and asked him where he lived.

"Down to Stillwater, New York," he told her. "I've one of Major Bleeker's farms."

Mrs. Powell burst into laughter at that. She was American born and Major Bleeker was her father. For the War of 1812, fought back and forth across the Canadian border, was very much a civil war in which families who had known each other for generations found themselves opposed.

As night deepened, silence fell over the occupied town. Only in the garrison hospital was there activity. There, scores of desperately wounded men from both sides screamed without let-up into the darkness. An American soldier's mate, Dr. William Beaumont, had seen death, but the ghastly scene before him broke his heart – the men groaning and screaming, the surgeons wading in blood, "severing limbs with knife and saw or trepanning shattered skulls." The most hardened assassin, the cruelest savage, Beaumont thought, would be shocked at the spectacle. For forty-eight hours, without food or sleep, the young doctor cut and slashed, sickened by the carnage of war.

In his eyes, these mashed and mangled men were no longer friends or enemies, only fellow creatures. Nobody, he thought, could view such a spectacle without the blood chilling in his veins; none could behold it without agonizing sympathy.

The following morning, John Strachan, angered because the Americans had not agreed to the terms of surrender, demanded to see Dearborn himself. The American general was in a bad humour, clearly nonplussed by the presumption of this cleric badgering him over minor details of a surrender the general considered a *fait accompli*.

Strachan brandished the articles of surrender, still unsigned. Dearborn glanced at the document without comment. Strachan persisted. When would Dearborn parole the officers and men of the militia? When would he allow the townspeople to care for their sick and wounded? Dearborn's irritation grew. Who were the conquered here? Who the conqueror? Who was the strange civilian with the thick Scots burr who seemed to think he could deal with generals? He told Strachan, harshly, that the Americans had been given a false return of the captured officers, and then warned him away.

But Strachan was not to be shoved aside. He wouldn't be duped, he said, or insulted. Either the document would be signed at once, or it would not be signed at all. There would be *no* capitulation! Let the Americans do their worst! With that he turned on his heel and walked back to the garrison.

These rough tactics were successful. Dearborn, in a better humour, signed the document. The militia were paroled and the community began to return to something resembling normality. But the Americans threatened to burn the town if the public funds, which had been concealed, were not given up. They managed to get the paper money but not the gold. A young clerk, dressed up as a market woman, complete with sun-bonnet and flowing skirts, was spirited out of town with the precious metal loaded onto a one-horse wagon and covered with vegetables.

When William Playter arrived back in town after hiding in Newmarket, he found the town plundered. The garrison buildings were shattered, the council office stripped bare, every window broken. The legislative building, a low one-storey brick structure with two wings, one for each house, was ablaze. No one knew who set the fire. The Americans were blamed without any hard evidence. The best guess is that the culprits were individual American sailors who wore no uniforms.

Although the upper class in York was opposed to the American invasion, scores of ordinary citizens either welcomed it or accepted it. For every man concealing himself to escape parole, there seemed to be another eager to sign a paper that would take him out of the war. A number joined the enemy. When it became clear that the Americans intended to leave town, panic seized those who supported the invaders, some of whom urged the American officers to hold on to York and give them protection.

Suspicion and sedition went hand in hand, as neighbour broke with neighbour over idle remarks or disloyal outbursts. In Michael Dye's tavern in Markham township, Alfred Barrett offered a toast: "Success to the American fleet!" Two friends raised their glasses in agreement. They were overheard by another, who also heard two others agree that it was foolish to support the government of Upper Canada. The country, they said, really belonged to the U.S. and they hoped the Americans would win. All four eventually found themselves in the York jail, charged with sedition.

Another man, Elijah Bentley, an Anabaptist preacher, was jailed for telling friends he had seen more liberty during the four hours of the Americans in York than he had seen in the whole of the province.

The Americans also made themselves popular with some farmers by distributing a number of farm implements that had been sent out by Britain and intended for the settlers but, as the result of bureaucratic inertia, never distributed. Many were convinced that the ruling class was reserving all that treasure for its friends.

Strachan's church was looted. Lawlessness prevailed. Once again the tireless clergyman went after the hard-pressed Dearborn. Now, all the American general wanted to do was to get out of York. There was no advantage in holding the town. The brig in the harbour was destroyed. The public stores destined for the frontier had been captured. All the arms and equipment for the British squadron on Lake Erie had been seized and couldn't be replaced. That loss would badly cripple the British right division, which held Detroit and most of Michigan Territory. It could, in fact, affect the balance of naval power on Lake Erie where the Americans were building another fleet.

If the Americans could win Lake Erie, Detroit would be regained, and the entire right wing of the British army in peril. For the Americans that was the plus side of the triumph at Little York.

But Dearborn was embarrassed by the continued looting which made a mockery of the terms of surrender. He realized he couldn't control his own troops and wanted nothing more than to leave as soon as the fleet was ready. He was only too happy to turn civilian control of the town back to the magistrates.

On May 1 the fleet made ready to sail. A storm kept the troops trapped and seasick on board the fleet for the best part of the week. The fourteen hundred troops that attacked York were reduced through injury, illness, and death to one thousand effective fighting men, but reinforcements were on their way. Dearborn expected six hundred men to join him at Oswego and more at Buffalo, while another thousand were waiting at Sackets Harbor.

For the people of York, the invasion marked a watershed. Nothing could ever be quite the same again. Those who fought the good fight with weapons or with words would occupy a special place in the community – especially Strachan, who became one of the leaders of the future. The lines were drawn. Those who aided the Americans, by word as much as by deed, were seen as traitors.

The militia, though it saw little action, were the darlings of the community. The regulars, who bore the brunt of the fighting, were criticized as men who cared only about saving their skins. That was completely unfair. Seven eminent citizens berated Sheaffe, whose name "is odious to all ranks of people." Strachan wrote the citizens were "indignant rather than dispirited and while they feel the disgrace of their defeat they console themselves with a conviction that it was owing entirely to their commander." His message to the Governor General, Sir George Prevost, was blunt: "Sheaffe must go."

Prevost couldn't agree with that armchair assessment, especially as neither the chaplain of York nor any of his colleagues could suggest what they might have done in the circumstances. But the Governor General was a practical politician and a diplomat. Sheaffe had outlived his usefulness. He was not sent back as an administrator. Eventually he was replaced by a Swiss-born major-general, Francis De Rottenburg. That was two months in the future. In the meantime, without any official rank, but all the power he needed, John Strachan reigned supreme.

CHAPTER THREE

The fall of Fort George

FOLLOWING THE ATTACK on York, the Americans decided on an immediate landing at the mouth of the Niagara river to seize Fort George, near the present site of Niagara-on-the-Lake. The plan was to seize the defending army and then roll up the entire Niagara peninsula. For this they had sixteen warships and seven thousand men. The British had eighteen hundred regular soldiers spread along the Niagara frontier. Most of the militia, however, had returned to their farms – for it was that kind of war, when men ploughed the fields one day and shouldered a musket the next.

Major-General Dearborn, ill and indecisive, dallied for a fortnight before launching his invasion. It came on May 27, 1813.

Like John Strachan before him, Brigadier-General John Vincent, the commander of the fort, looked out that morning at another alarming spectacle.

The curtain of fog lifted, as in a theatre, and there was now revealed to him and his staff a spectacle he would never forget – sixteen ships standing out from the lake-shore sweeping toward him in a two-mile (3 km) arc. Behind them on tow lines, 134 open boats, scows, and bateaux, crowded with men and artillery, moved steadily toward the Canadian side.

Now the cannon began to thunder – fifty-one guns in action on the lake, and another twenty from the American Fort Niagara across the river, pouring a hail of iron and exploding shells across the fields and roads. The barrage was so powerful that the people of York, forty miles (65

As the curtain of fog lifted at Fort George, a large American fleet, moving toward the Canadian side, came into plain view.

km) across the lake, distinctly heard the rumble of the guns.

The enemy was manoeuvring to catch the British batteries in a crossfire and the effect was shattering. One battery at the lighthouse managed to get off a single shot before it was destroyed. Another at Two Mile Creek to the west had to be abandoned. As the fleet continued its majestic movement forward, three schooners moved close to the shore to cover the landing at Cookstown, a huddle of farmhouses near the mouth of Two Mile Creek.

In a thicket overlooking this potential invasion point, Vincent had hidden a guard of fifty Mohawk under their celebrated Scottish chief, John Norton. A hail of missiles fired at point blank range pierced the hiding place, killing two Indians and wounding several others before the main body fled.

On board his flagship, General Dearborn, still too ill to lead the attack himself, watched nervously as the assault boats moved toward the shore.

He could see a young naval officer, Oliver Hazard Perry, directing the fire from an open boat, standing tall in the stern, in full uniform, ignoring enemy musket fire. He was rowed from vessel to vessel telling each where to anchor to achieve the best field of fire. With that done, he boarded the *Madison*, determined to have nothing further to do with the invasion, which he believed to be badly planned and poorly carried out. He was eager for action, but his advice was ignored, and he had no intention of taking the blame for any disasters that might result.

Then he had a sudden change of heart. The one man he admired, Colonel Winfield Scott, Dearborn's adjutant-general, was in danger. Perry saw that he was being blown off course in the leading flatboat and was about to miss the landing point. Perry begged to be allowed to avert that disaster, leaped into his boat, picked up Scott and with his help herded the scattered assault craft back on course. At that point a lookout on the mast of the schooner, *Hamil-*

ton, shouted that the whole British Army was advancing on the double to block the landing.

Most of the American officers didn't believe the British would make a stand. That view was reinforced by a high bank which concealed the defending troops. But Perry sensed danger. He set off to warn Scott, slipping in and out between the advancing ships. As he reached the lead assault boat, the British fired a volley. Confusion followed. The soldiers began firing wildly in every direction. Perry, fearing they would shoot each other, yelled to them to row to shore.

Scott echoed the order. He was in charge of twenty boats containing eight hundred men and a three-pound (1.4 kg) cannon. He ordered his men to advance three hundred paces across the beach and then wait for the first wave of infantry – fifteen hundred troops under Brigadier-General John Boyd.

Into the water they went, through the spray and onto the sand. As they dashed for the bank, the next wave approached the beach. The water turned to foam under the torrent of musketry.

At the same time, Scott's assault force reached the crest of the twelve-foot (4 m) clay bank. The British hurled them back down the cliff. Scott – a gigantic figure, six feet, five inches (2 m) tall – was unmistakable. One of the Glengarrys attacked him with a bayonet but Scott dodged away, lost his footing and tumbled back down the bank.

Dearborn, on board the *Madison*, saw this and uttered an agonizing cry:

"He is lost! He is killed!"

But Scott picked himself up and led a second charge up the bank. The British retreated to the cover of the ravine. Then Lieutenant-Colonel Christopher Myers, Vincent's acting quartermaster-general, led a second attack and Scott was again forced back.

Now two lines of men faced each other at a distance of no more than ten yards (9 m). For the next fifteen minutes they fired away at point-blank range, and a scene of carnage followed. On the British side every field officer and most junior officers were casualties. The British were forced back, leaving a hundred corpses piled on the bank. An American surgeon counted four hundred dead and wounded men strewn over a plot no longer than two hundred yards (180 m) and no broader than fifteen (14 m).

As reinforcements arrived, the British retreated stubbornly from ravine to ravine back toward the little town of Newark. By now with more troops landing on the beach, and another American column massing farther up the river, Vincent realized that nothing could save the fort.

With tears in his eyes, he sent a note ordering that the magazine be blown up, and the garrison evacuate the fort to rejoin the retreating army on the Queenston Road.

The British retreated swiftly and silently toward the village of St. Davids as a main magazine blew up, hurling a crowd of debris into the air and causing a piece of timber to knock Scott off his horse and break his collarbone. But the Americans were in danger of winning another hollow victory and Scott knew it – for the British were melting away. He hoisted his big frame back on his injured horse and galloped off in the wake of his own troops, who were already picking up British stragglers.

Scott did not reckon on the timidity of his commanding officer. Dearborn couldn't make a decision. He turned direct command over to Major-General Morgan Lewis, a politician, not a soldier, who loved playing commander and revelled in pomp and ceremony, but was terrified of making a mistake.

Lewis sent two messengers forward to restrain Scott, who was eager to bag the British. Scott had to abandon his plans, under a direct order to withdraw to Fort George. He could see the rear guard of the British army disappearing into the woods. The defeated columns were marching off in perfect order with much of their equipment intact, which lessened the American triumph. Once again the invaders had cracked the shell of the nut, but lost the kernel. Trapped all year in Fort George, unable to break out for long because of Vincent's raiders lurking on the outskirts, an entire American army would shortly be reduced to illness, idleness, and frustration.

Dearborn's immediate instinct was to move his troops to the head of the lake by water and cut off the British retreat. For that venture, he needed the enthusiastic cooperation of the fleet and its commodore, Isaac Chauncey, aged forty-one –

Colonel Winfield Scott leads a second charge up the bank.

a pear-shaped figure with a pear-shaped head, double-chin, and sleepy eyes. The navy had been Chauncey's life. He was determined to win naval superiority on Lake Ontario. It was this that obsessed him more than anything else. As he saw it, his task was to build as many ships as possible and then preserve them from attack, and to destroy the enemy's fleet. But the fear of losing the contest, and thus losing the lake, made him wary and overcautious.

Chauncey did not dare. Before he attacked the British flotilla, everything had to be right – wind, weather, naval superiority. But since nothing could ever be quite right for Chauncey, this war would be a series of frustrations. He and his equally cautious opposite number, Sir James Yeo, flitted about the lake, avoiding decisive action – always waiting for the right moment, which never came.

Finally, word came that a British fleet was at the other end of the lake attacking Sackets Harbor. That attack failed, but the Americans panicked. They briefly set fire to their own partially-built warship, *General Pike*, thus delaying its launch date. That was enough for Chauncey who left the Niagara frontier, taking all his ships and two thousand troops. It was a withdrawal that allowed Vincent's army to reach the protection of the heights above Burlington Bay (near the present city of Hamilton). If the Americans were to dislodge them, they would have to proceed by land.

N OW THE GREATER part of the Niagara peninsula was in American hands. The invaders, having seized Fort George at the mouth of the Niagara and also Fort Erie, some thirty miles (50 km) up-river, were advancing toward the Burlington heights. There, Vincent's small force of seven hundred regulars were dug in. But how could he hold out against three thousand Americans?

None of that concerned young Billy Green, a high-spirited youth of nineteen, living near Stoney Creek, not far from Burlington. For Billy, the war was a lark. When he and his older brother, Levi, heard the Americans were only a few kilometres away, they couldn't restrain their excitement. They simply had to have a good look at the advancing army.

Billy was the youngest of Adam Green's seven children. Left motherless almost at birth, he was known as a loner and a woodsman who could shinny up any tree and swing from branch to branch like a monkey. Now, at six o'clock on the humid spring morning of June 5, he and Levi clambered up the Niagara escarpment and made their way south until they reached a point above the American camp at the mouth of Forty Mile Creek.

That noon, hidden from view, they watched the Americans marching by and waited until almost all had passed. Then they began to yell like Indians – a sound that sent a chill through the stragglers.

"I tell you, those simple fellows did run," is the way Billy described it.

They scampered back along the ridge and then scrambled down to the road the soldiers had just passed over. There they ran into one lone American, one boot off, tying a rag onto his blistered foot. When he went for his musket, Levi Green hit him with a stick. The resulting yells of pain drew a rattle of musket fire from the rear guard. At that the brothers dashed back up the slope, whooping like Indians, until they reached Levi Green's cabin on a piece of bench land.

The sound of war whoops and gunfire drew several settlers from their homes. A small crowd looked down from the brow of the hill at the Americans marching through the village of Stoney Creek – a scattered huddle of log cabins and taverns. Some of the marchers halted long enough to fire at the hill. One musket ball came so close it struck a fence rail directly in front of Levi's wife, Tina, who was holding their oldest child, Hannah, in her arms.

Now the brothers went down to the village, where their sister, Kezia Corman, told them the Americans had taken her husband, Isaac, a prisoner. Billy started off at a dead run across Stoney Creek, whistling for his brother-in-law. A few moments later he heard an owl hoot and knew it was Isaac. The missing man had made his escape by pretending to be friendly to the American cause – a believable enough pretence in this province.

Isaac simply told the major that captured him that he was a Kentuckian. And the major promptly let him go. When Corman explained he couldn't get through the American lines, his captor gave him the countersign of the day. It was Wil-Hen-Har – the first syllables of the name of the American general, William Henry Harrison.

Billy Green now owned a vital piece of information. He knew what he had to do. He had to get a message to the British at Burlington. He borrowed his brother's horse, Tip, and rode him as far as he could. Then he tied him to a fence and made his way to the British lines on foot.

At that very hour the British were planning to gamble on a night raid on the American camp. Lieutenant-Colonel John Harvey had already scouted the American position and thought it vulnerable. He was by far the most experienced officer in the division. At thirty-four, he was thirteen years younger than his commander, Vincent, and had spent more than half his life in active service around the world.

The hawk-faced Harvey was a firm believer in accurate information bought at any price, and also in a series of bold and active offensive moves to throw the enemy on the defensive. Now he acted on these two convictions. He had not only scouted the enemy himself, but one of his subalterns, James FitzGibbon of the 49th, an especially bold and enterprising officer, had disguised himself as a butter pedlar and actually entered the American camp to observe the location of troops and guns.

Harvey, then, was able to report that the Americans were badly scattered, their cannon was poorly placed, and their cavalry too far in the rear to be useful. He urged an immediate attack by night at bayonet point. It was their only chance, for ammunition was low; the American fleet might arrive at any moment.

Now, thanks to young Billy Green, Harvey had the countersign. He asked Billy if he knew the way to the American camp.

"Every inch of it," replied Billy proudly.

Harvey gave him a corporal's sword, which Billy kept for the rest of his long life, and told him to take the lead. It was eleven-thirty. The troops, sleeping on the grass, were aroused and the column set off on a seven-mile (11 km) march through the black night. It was so dark the men could scarcely see each other. The moon was masked by heavy clouds. The tall pines added to the gloom. A soft mist blurred the trails. Only the occasional flash of heat lightning relieved the blackness.

The soldiers plodded forward in silence, their footfalls muffled by the mud of the trail. Harvey had cautioned against uttering so much as a whisper. Even the flints had been removed from the firelocks to prevent the accidental

Billy Green, corporal's sword in hand, leads the British troops to the Americans' position at Stoney Creek.

firing of a musket. Billy Green, loping on ahead, found he had left the column behind and had to retrace his steps to urge more speed – otherwise it would be daylight before the quarry was flushed. Well, someone in the ranks was heard to mutter, that would be soon enough to be killed.

By three, on this sultry Sunday morning, Harvey's force reached the first American sentry post. Later, nobody could remember the exact order of events that followed, someone fired a musket. One sentry at least was quietly bayonetted. Another demanded the countersign and Billy Green gave it to him, at the same time seizing his gun with one hand and killing him with his new sword held in the other.

An American advance party of fifty men, quartered in a church, were overpowered and taken prisoner. The Americans were camped on a low grassy meadow through which a branch of Stoney Creek trickled. The main road ran over the creek and climbed the ridge. Its crest was marked by a tangle of trees and roots behind which most of the American infantry and guns were located.

The British could see the glow of the American campfires directly ahead. Moving forward to bayonet the sleeping enemy, they discovered to their disappointment that the meadow was empty. The Americans had left their cooking fires earlier to take up a stronger position on the ridge.

Now the attackers fixed flints. But all hope of surprise was lost, because they were easily spotted in the campfire glow. As they dashed forward whooping like the Indians to terrify the enemy, they were met by a sheet of flame. All was confusion. The musket smoke added to the thickness of the night, and the howls of the British mingled with the sinister *click click click* of muskets being reloaded. All sense of formation was lost. As some fled, others advanced, and friend had difficulty distinguishing foe in the darkness.

The enterprising FitzGibbon, seeing the men retreating on the left, ran along the line to restore order. The left flank held. Five hundred Americans were put to flight. But on their right the British were being pushed back by more than two thousand men. The guns on the ridge were doing heavy damage. But as Harvey had guessed, the Americans' centre was weak, because the guns did not have close infantry support.

Major Charles Plenderleath of the 49th realized his men had no chance unless the guns were captured. He called for volunteers. Alexander Fraser, a huge sergeant, only nineteen years old, gathered twenty men and with his commander sprinted up the road to rush the guns. Two volleys roared over their heads, but before the gunners could reload they were bayonetted. Plenderleath and Fraser cut right through, driving all before them, stabbing horses and men with crazy abandon. The American line was cut, four of six guns captured, and one hundred prisoners seized.

The American commander, Brigadier-General John Chandler, a former blacksmith, tavern keeper, and congressman, received his appointment because of political influence rather than military experience, of which he had none. He was up at the first musket shot, galloping about on his horse, shouting orders, trying to rally his scattered troops. He spent the rest of his life defending his actions that night.

His horse stumbled, threw him to the ground, and knocked him senseless. By the time he recovered, all was confusion. He saw a group of men by the guns, which to his dismay did not seem to be firing. He rushed forward, mistaking the men of the British 49th for his own, realized his error too late, tried to hide under a gun carriage, and was quickly hauled out by Sergeant Fraser, who made him prisoner.

His second-in-command, William Winder, a former Baltimore lawyer and another political appointee, was also lost. He was about to fire when Fraser appeared. "If you stir, you die," said the sergeant. Winder threw down his pistol and his sword and surrendered.

The American command now fell to the cavalry officer, Colonel James Burns, whose troops were too far in the rear to be effective during the attack. Burns and his horsemen roared down on the British, cut through the lines and opened fire, only to find they were shooting at their own comrades who were wandering about firing at one another. Friend and foe were now entangled, both sides taking prisoners and neither knowing how the battle was going. Vincent himself was knocked from his horse and separated from his staff, lost somewhere in the woods, stumbling about in the wrong direction.

Each force left the field believing the other victorious.

Harvey decided to withdraw without Vincent before the Americans could recover from their confusion. But the Americans were also preparing to flee, as William Hamilton Merritt, the leader of the volunteer dragoons, discovered when he rode back to the field shortly after dawn, seeking his missing commander. He was able to report the Americans were in a panic, destroying everything that couldn't be removed. In their haste, they didn't even stop to bury their dead.

The British returned to the Stoney Creek battlefield that afternoon to find guns, stores, and baggage still scattered about the field among the litter of the dead. Vincent turned up last, exhausted and half-famished, his sword, hat and horse missing.

The American retreat continued. Dearborn, at Fort George, ordered Morgan Lewis to attack the British again at Stoney Creek. But Lewis moved so slowly that he was of little use. Meanwhile the British fleet, under Sir James Yeo, appeared outside the mouth of the Niagara river apparently threatening Fort George. Dearborn sent a note to Lewis to get back as fast as he could.

As the British vessels moved up to Forty Mile Creek, Lewis retired, abandoning his supplies in such haste that the occupying British seized six hundred tents, two hundred camp kettles, one hundred and forty barrels of flour, one hundred and fifty muskets, and a baggage train of twenty boats for which the Americans had neglected to supply an escort.

Within three days of the battle of Stoney Creek, the situation along the Niagara frontier had been reversed. The Americans had been in full possession of the peninsula, outnumbering the British defenders at least three-to-one. The command at Montreal was prepared to evacuate most of the province, to sacrifice the militia, and pull back the regulars to Kingston. But as the result of a single unequal contest, hastily planned at the last moment and fought in absolute darkness by confused and disorganized men, the invaders had lost control.

On June 9, the Americans burned Fort Erie and evacuated all the defence posts along the Niagara river, retiring in a body behind the log palisades of Fort George. Except for a few brief raids, that would be their prison until winter forced them back across the river to American soil.

CHAPTER FIVE

Laura Secord's journey

THE AMERICANS WERE bottled up in Fort George and the British meant to keep them there. The Americans, on their part, wanted to burst out and make another attempt to seize the Niagara Peninsula. And so the war, that summer of 1813, became a secret war. Soldiers from both armies, often disguised as civilians, sometimes pretending to be on the opposite side, crept through the forests to launch lightning attacks against their former neighbours. Civilians, too, battled civilians and, since everybody spoke the same language, it was difficult to tell friend from foe.

Lieutenant James FitzGibbon headed a troop of British mounted soldiers ("dragoons") known as "The Bloody Boys" and disguised as civilians. At the same time, an American surgeon, Dr. Cyrenius Chapin, rode at the head of a body of American mounted volunteers, plundering the homes of Canadian settlers. Chapin was a medical man who had once practised on the Canadian side of the border and so knew most of his adversaries by sight.

FitzGibbon was determined to stop Chapin and his forays. On June 21 he left his men hidden near Lundy's Lane, not far from Niagara Falls, and moved up the road on his own seeking information about Chapin's movements. He spotted a fluttering handkerchief waved by Mrs. James Kerby, the wife of a local militia captain, who ran to him and urged him to flee. Chapin, she told him, had just passed through at the head of two hundred men.

FitzGibbon had no intention of running away. He spotted an enemy's horse hitched to a post in front of Deffield's Inn. He rode up, dismounted, and burst in. An American rifleman covered him, but FitzGibbon, who was wearing a grey-green overall over his uniform as a disguise, clasped him by the hand, claiming they were old friends. Having thus thrown the enemy off guard, he seized his rifle barrel and ordered him to surrender.

The man refused and clung to his own weapon, trying to fire it while his comrade levelled his own piece at FitzGibbon. FitzGibbon turned about, kept the first rifle clamped in his right hand, caught the other's with his left and forced it down until it pointed at his comrade. Now he exercised his great strength to drag both men out of the tavern, all three swearing and calling on one another to surrender.

Up ran Mrs. Kerby, begging and threatening. Up scampered a small boy, who hurled rocks at the Americans. The trio continued to struggle, until one of the Americans managed to pull FitzGibbon's sword from its sheath. But just as he was about to thrust it into his opponent's chest, Mrs.

Deffield, the tavern keeper's wife, kicked the weapon out of his hand.

FitzGibbon threw one of his assailants against the steps and disarmed him. The other was attacked by the tavern keeper. FitzGibbon mounted his horse and, driving his two prisoners before him, made his escape before Chapin's main force arrived.

At this point the Niagara Peninsula was a no man's land. The populace was split between those loyal to the British cause and the others who had flocked to the American side. For most people the best policy was to lie low and try to keep out of trouble. But there were some who were prepared to risk their lives to harass the Americans. It was FitzGibbon's task to aid these partisans and help keep the enemy off balance and penned up in Fort George by ambushes and skirmishes. His fifty volunteers were disguised in the same grey-green coveralls and trained in guerrilla warfare. FitzGibbon was the perfect leader for such a force – a popular officer, unconventional, immensely strong and lithe.

The day after he escaped from Cyrenius Chapin's marauders, FitzGibbon took his men to the two-storey stone house owned by a militia captain, John De Cew, not far from Beaver Dams on Twelve Mile Creek, about seventeen miles (27 km) from Fort George.

The De Cew house formed the apex of a triangle of defence the British had thrown out to keep the Americans bottled up at Fort George. At the left base of the triangle, seven miles (11 km) away at the mouth of Twelve Mile Creek, Major Peter De Haren was stationed with three companies of regulars. At the right base, farther up the lake on the heights above Twenty Mile Creek, Lieutenant-Colonel Cecil Bisshopp was posted with a small brigade of light infantry. Merritt's provincial dragoons, FitzGibbon's Bloody Boys, Norton's Mohawks and Captain Dominique Ducharme's band of Caughnawaga Indians patrolled the intervening countryside.

It was all very romantic – men on horseback, often disguised, riding at night, cutting and thrusting, taking prisoners, making hairbreadth escapes. But for those whose homes were plundered and whose menfolk were killed and wounded, it was also tragic.

Then, on June 23 just after sunset, a Canadian legend was born. A slight and delicate little Loyalist arrived at the De Cew house to announce that she had an important message for FitzGibbon. This was Mrs. James Secord – Laura Secord – aged thirty-eight, wife of a militia man badly wounded at the Battle of Queenston Heights, and mother of five.

Mrs. Secord told FitzGibbon that she had heard from Americans in Queenston that an attack was being planned on the De Cew headquarters the following day. To carry her warning, she had made her way on foot through the dreaded Black Swamp that lay between Queenston and De Cew's house, staying clear of the main roads in order to avoid capture. She was exhausted but game, triumphant after her long journey, which had apparently taken her, at some risk, through the camp of the Caughnawagas.

Mrs. Secord's warning caused FitzGibbon to alert Norton's Mohawks to keep his men posted all night to warn of an impending attack. None came. Was her story then a fabrication? Hardly. She was the daughter of a Loyalist family. Her husband was still crippled from wounds caused by American soldiers. She hadn't struggled nineteen miles (30 km) in the boiling sun from Queenston, through St. Davids and across a treacherous morass, on a whim.

But there was a mystery to all this. Laura Secord never made it clear exactly how she had heard the rumour of an impending attack on the afternoon or evening of June 21. She was vague and contradictory about this detail, telling FitzGibbon that her husband learned of it from an American officer, but telling her granddaughter years later that she herself overheard it.

Her exhausting journey was even more baffling because it was undertaken on the thinnest evidence – an unproven rumour, flimsy as gossamer. On June 21 the Americans had

Laura Secord arrives at the De Cew house bearing an important message for Lieutenant FitzGibbon.

yet to make any firm plans to attack De Cew's headquarters. Even Lieutenant-Colonel Charles Boerstler, the man chosen to lead the eventual attack, didn't know of it until the afternoon of June 23.

Who were those Americans in Queenston on June 21? They must have been Chapin's followers, for the regular troops had been called back to Fort George for fear of being cut off. Yet Chapin, by his own statement, knew nothing of any attack and would not hear of it until the orders were issued on June 23.

Yet *something* was in the wind. Had someone whispered a warning in Mrs. Secord's ear? Who? It was not in her interest to give her source. News travelled on wings on the Niagara frontier. Who knew what damage might be done if Laura revealed what she knew? Her invalid husband and children could easily be the objects of revenge on this peninsula of tangled loyalties.

Like everybody else who lived along the border, the Secords had friends on both sides. Before the war the people moved freely between the two countries, buying and selling, owning land, operating businesses without regard to nationality. Chapin's men were virtually neighbours. The Secords would have known most of them.

It may be that, in later years, when the past became fuzzy, Mrs. Secord simply couldn't remember the details of her source, though she seems to have remembered everything else. It was equally possible that she refused to identify her informant to save him and his descendants from the harsh whispers and bitter scandal of treason.

For all of her long life, Laura Secord told her story many times, adding to it more than once. A cow became part of the legend although, in truth, there never was a cow.

Her story was used to underline the growing myth that the War of 1812 was won by true-blue Canadians – in this case a brave Loyalist housewife who single-handedly saved the British army from defeat. That was an exaggeration but it fitted neatly with John Strachan's own conviction that the Canadian militia, and not the British regulars or the Indians, were the real heroes.

CHAPTER SIX

The Battle of Beaver Dams

COOPED UP IN Fort George, the ailing American general, Henry Dearborn, knew he must do something to restore his shattered reputation. The enemy had escaped him at Fort York and beaten him at Stoney Creek. Now FitzGibbon's mounted marauders were creating havoc along the peninsula.

Dearborn decided to mount a massive excursion to wipe out the Bloody Boys. He had just learned that FitzGibbon had made his headquarters at the De Cew house. He figured that five hundred men and two guns, guided by Chapin and his followers, could do the job.

He turned the details over to his second-in-command, Brigadier-General John Boyd, a former soldier-of-fortune. Boyd was no more popular than his predecessor, Morgan Lewis, who thought him a bully and a show-off and who had warned against just the sort of attack that Boyd and Dearborn were now contemplating.

In fact, the command at Fort George was torn with petty jealousies. There was little love lost between Dr. Chapin, who would guide the expedition, and the officer chosen to lead it, Lieutenant-Colonel Charles Boerstler. Boerstler was a thirty-five-year-old regular from Maryland, who despised the self-appointed civilian leader. Yet the surgeon appeared to be the more war-like of the two. The sallow-faced Boerstler was unusually sensitive to imagined insults. Chapin was a lithe six-footer with a great beak of a nose and piercing blue eyes, known for his boldness as well as for his ego. He couldn't stand Boerstler, whom he called "a broken down Methodist preacher." Boerstler in his turn had no use for Chapin, whom he called "a vain and boasting liar."

Nor did Boerstler like either Boyd or Winfield Scott, both of whom had been involved in what he considered insults to his abilities. Chapin tried to put off Boerstler's appointment, but the high command, knowing Boerstler to be touchy, wasn't prepared to offend him.

The expedition was hastily and imperfectly planned. No attempt was made to divert the posts at the other two corners of the defensive triangle, while De Cew's house was being attacked. There was no reserve on which Boerstler could fall back in case of disaster. The problem was the lack of men – half the army being too sick to fight. Boerstler had been promised a body of riflemen, essential in the kind of bush fighting that was certain to take place, but these sharpshooters were needed for guard duty. He marched off without them.

Boerstler sent patrols to prevent any citizen from escaping with news of the troops' advance. (Laura Secord had

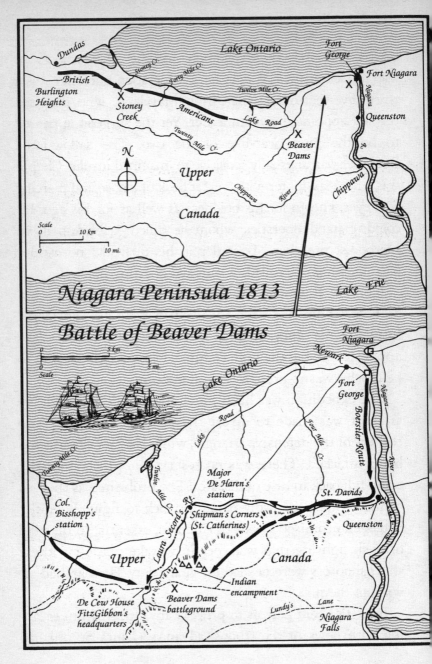

Niagara Peninsula 1813

Battle of Beaver Dams

been at FitzGibbon's headquarters for more than twenty-four hours) At daybreak the detachment moved on to St. Davids, where it surprised two Caughnawagas. One was shot, but the other escaped to warn Major De Haren of the Americans' advance.

The Americans moved in a column up the side of the Niagara escarpment, halted at the top, moved on again for about a kilometre past an open field and into a narrow ravine bordered on both sides by thick woods. It was here that the Battle of Beaver Dams began.

Francis Dominique Ducharme, a forty-eight-year-old veteran of twenty-five years' service in the western fur country, was the leader of the Caughnawaga Indians. He persuaded De Haren to allow him to move out of his original position, in order to ambush the Americans in the woods. The Indians killed every one of Chapin's advance guard at the outset of the battle.

Boerstler ordered his wagons and horses to the rear, out of the enemy fire, formed up Chapin's men, and led a charge against the Indians – a charge made futile by his lack of experienced sharpshooters.

To Chapin he was a blunderer. It was Chapin who, according to his later account, foresaw the Indian ambush and warned his commander. He was in the act of driving the natives through the woods, when he was called back against his will by the timid and hesitant Boerstler.

There were several versions of the Battle of Beaver Dams, but one thing was clear. By noon the attacking troops were exhausted. Boerstler, feeling hemmed in by the woods and the hidden Indians, had made the mistake of leading his men forward and keeping them for too long under heavy fire. In fact, his detachment was too small and his plans imperfect and hurried. The troops had been up since dawn, had marched eleven miles (18 km) without refreshment, had fought for three hours under the blazing sun, and had exhausted their ammunition.

At that moment, James FitzGibbon appeared on the scene, carrying a white flag and demanding an American surrender. He had actually been in the area for some time. He had been alerted in the morning, by Ducharme's Caughnawaga scouts, to the presence of an enemy column advancing on his post. He had scouted the battle fields and sent for his men. But he could not depend on the Indians, who were coming and going on whim. No one was capable of forcing a surrender, and Ducharme couldn't speak English. So FitzGibbon decided upon a bluff and strode forward, white flag in hand.

Boerstler sent his artillery captain, McDowell, to meet him. The two parleyed. FitzGibbon resorted to a tried and true threat. He said he had been dispatched by Major De Haren to inform the Americans that they were surrounded by a superior force of British, that they couldn't escape, and that the Indians were infuriated to the point of massacre. But Boerstler refused to surrender. He wasn't accustomed, he said, to surrender to an army he hadn't seen.

FitzGibbon's bluff had been called. There was no unseen army – only Ducharme and his Caughnawagas. Nonetheless, FitzGibbon boldly proposed that the Americans send an officer to examine De Haren's force. That would convince them that the odds against them were overwhelming, he said. Boerstler agreed, but declared he would not surrender unless he found himself badly outnumbered. FitzGibbon then retired to pretend that he was consulting with De Haren who wasn't anywhere near the scene. Instead he ran into Captain John Hall who had just ridden up with a dozen provincial dragoons. FitzGibbon persuaded him to impersonate the absent major.

Back he went to report that De Haren had agreed to receive one of the American officers. Boerstler sent a subaltern, who encountered Hall, thinking him to be De Haren. Hall, thinking quickly, declared that it would be humiliating to display his force, but insisted it was quite large enough to compel surrender. Boerstler, weak from loss of blood from wounds sustained in the battle, asked for time to decide. FitzGibbon gave him five minutes, explaining he couldn't control his Indians much longer.

"For God's sake," cried Boerstler, "keep the Indians from us!" And with the spectacle of massacre never far from his mind, he agreed to surrender.

FitzGibbon now faced a problem. How could his tiny force disarm five hundred of the enemy without his deception being discovered – especially when the real Major De

Haren was nowhere to be found? Fortunately a more senior officer, Lieutenant-Colonel John Clark, arrived, followed shortly after by De Haren himself with a body of troops.

But FitzGibbon had one other problem. He must explain his deception to De Haren before the Major unwittingly revealed it to the enemy. In addition, he wanted credit for the surrender and feared that De Haren would rob him of it. To his discomfiture, De Haren brushed him aside. He was clearly about to offer surrender conditions on his own to Boerstler.

At this, FitzGibbon stepped up quickly, laid his hand on the neck of the major's horse, and spoke in a low, firm voice:

"Not another word, sir; these are my prisoners."

Then he stepped back and cried loudly, "Shall I disarm the American troops?"

To that De Haren had to agree.

FitzGibbon still feared the major, by some remark, might ruin everything. The Americans could easily overwhelm them if the deception was revealed. He quickly ordered the troops into file and, as soon as some were formed, rapped out an order to the men to march, thus driving Boerstler and De Haren forward to prevent conversation between them.

The marching Americans, still armed, were rapidly approaching FitzGibbon's small force of Bloody Boys. He suggested to De Haren that the captives ground arms at once.

"No," said De Haren harshly, "let them march through between our men and ground their arms on the other side."

What folly! thought FitzGibbon. *When they see our handful, will they really ground their weapons?*

He turned to De Haren: "Do you think it prudent to march them through with arms in their hands in the presence of the Indians?"

At the mention of the dreaded word *Indians*, Boerstler threw up a hand, "For God's sake, sir, do what this officer bids you!"

De Haren agreed, the prisoners dropped their weapons, the Indians appeared from behind trees and bushes and rushed toward them. FitzGibbon, springing up on a stump, shouted that no one would be hurt and allowed the Indians to plunder the muskets, knives, swords, and other equipments.

The Battle of Beaver Dams had confirmed the inability of the invaders to break out of their prison at Fort George. Boerstler had lost more than five hundred men, including Chapin and twenty-one of his mounted corps. The big doctor wasn't a prisoner for long. Later on he succeeded in overpowering his captors and escaping.

Dearborn was stunned by the disaster, describing the Battle of Beaver Dams as "an unfortunate and unaccountable event." But generals must be accountable. When the news reached Washington, there was an immediate demand for the sick old soldier's removal. His officers urged him to move the army back to American soil, but a council of war agreed to hold fast. Dearborn, however, was himself removed, as much to his own relief as to that of his officers.

CHAPTER SEVEN

The second attack on York

P ANIC AGAIN STRUCK York at the end of July, 1813. Square sails were seen on the lake – white jibs, red stripes and blue stars flying from the stern. With a new American warship finally launched at Sackets Harbor, the naval balance on Lake Ontario had changed again. The Americans were back in force on this humid summer morning of July 31 – at least a dozen vessels nearing the harbour.

By the time the leading vessels anchored off the garrison, the town was all but empty of men. It was true that they had given their parole but they did not trust the Americans. Along the Niagara frontier other paroled military officers had been bundled up and taken across the border to captivity on foreign soil, and so the men of York were taking no chances.

William Allen, a merchant and militia major, reached the Playter farmhouse on north Yonge Street. There, with the help of Ely Playter and his brother, he concealed a boatload of five thousand cartridges and another crammed

William Allen and Ely Playter conceal cartridges from the attacking Americans in a marsh near the Don River.

with baggage in a marsh near the Don River. Then he moved north and hid out in the woods.

Through the silent streets of the empty town, two men made their way to the garrison. Grant Powell, the son of the chief justice, had elected to stay. And so, of course, had the Reverend Dr. Strachan. (Who would dare imprison *him*?) They reached the garrison about two o'clock and waited for developments.

They watched the largest vessels come to anchor at three o'clock. The wind was so light that the schooners, trailing behind, had to use their sweeps. At four, they saw the boats put off. Two hundred and fifty men landed without opposition. All the available British troops had long since retired to defend Burlington Heights.

Carrying a white flag, Strachan tackled the first officer to reach the shore and demanded to be taken to the commodore, Isaac Chauncey. With Winfield Scott at his elbow, Chauncey was cordial enough. Indeed, he expressed regret at the theft of the books from the library the previous April, said he had made a search of the fleet for these books, had found several and would return them. Strachan demanded to know what his intentions were. He pointed out that the present inhabitants of York were all women and children. Did he mean to destroy the community? If so, would he allow the removal of these noncombatants?

Chauncey reassured him. He planned no looting, only the seizure of public stores, and the burning of all fortifications. The major purpose of the expedition was retaliation for British attacks on the far side of the lake. He did not say it, but the real reason for the expedition, surely, was the need to do *something*. Cooped up in Sackets Harbor and Fort George, the Americans were denied a naval confrontation by the elusive British commodore, Sir James Yeo. Stalemated in their attempts to seize the Niagara peninsula, they needed action, any action.

Chauncey asked where the public stores were. Strachan and Powell would not tell him. It didn't matter because Chauncey already knew, or soon found out. He knew the state of York's defences. He knew the position of the army on Burlington Heights and knew every single transaction that had taken place in the town.

He also knew that some public stores had been hidden in William Allen's store, and that Allen, himself a militia officer under parole, had been collecting and sending information to the British army and aiding in the forwarding of troops. Winfield Scott offered a five hundred dollar reward for Allen's capture and sent his men to break into the store. They seized everything, broke open several officers' trunks, gave away the contents, and burned a large quantity of hemp. Others opened the jail and released all the prisoners. When Strachan attempted to protest to Scott, the American colonel brushed him off and declared he would seize all the provisions he could find.

In this he had the aid of a group of disloyal Canadians. One of them, John Lyon, brought his wagon down Yonge Street to help the Americans move the captured flour to the boat. His crony, Calvin Wood, jailed for sedition, was one of those released from the York jail. Wood and several others went aboard the American ships to give the enemy information; in gratitude, his new-found friends gave him seven barrels of flour.

From these informants Chauncey learned that boatloads of arms, baggage and ammunition had been hauled up the Don River. It was late in the evening. A half-hearted attempt to storm Burlington Heights had been called off. The fleet was about to leave. Now, however, the commodore postponed his departure. The following morning the troops disembarked, and three armed boats moved up the Don seeking the hidden supplies. But Ely Playter and his brother had already squirrelled most of them away, and the searchers returned disappointed.

The troops evacuated the town, burned the barracks and blockhouses, and returned to the ships. The fleet weighed anchor the following dawn and set sail for Sackets Harbor. Again, unaccountably, the Americans had decided not to occupy the capital and cut the line between Kingston and the British forces on the Niagara. The town breathed more freely. The inhabitants could not know that this was the last time a hostile flotilla would anchor in Toronto bay. The new centre of action would be on Lake Erie two hundred miles (320 km) to the southwest.

War passed York by, but its effects lingered on long after hostilities ended. John Lyon, Calvin Wood, and a clutch of other dissidents would soon find themselves in jail.

Charges of sedition and taunts of treason would be thrown at any who, by deed, word, or even gesture, appeared to support the American cause. It would no longer be wise to praise the American way of life.

A "committee of information" was about to come into being to take evidence from all loyal subjects who wished to inform on their neighbours. Its members were men of absolute loyalty and substance, the core of the Family Compact. For York – the future city of Toronto – the war was over. But in Upper Canada individual liberties were not a matter of pressing concern. Individualism, after all, was an American concept. "Liberty" was a Yankee word.

And so the campaign on the Niagara peninsula ended where it had begun some three months before – in stalemate. The American invaders were still hived in Fort George. The rest of Upper Canada was scarred but defiant. The war was by no means over, but for the settlers, desperately trying to preserve their fields of barley and wheat, hostilities had passed them by.

Index

COMING SOON

The start of a new series in Pierre Berton's
Adventures in Canadian History

BONANZA GOLD is the first book in *The Great Klondike Gold Rush*, a series devoted to the tumultuous events of the late nineteenth century when Canada's rugged, isolated Yukon Territory became the site of a frenzied gold stampede.

BONANZA GOLD tells the story of Robert Henderson, the guileless Nova Scotia prospector who, in 1896, made the first important gold discovery in the Klondike but failed to enjoy the riches he helped uncover. It's also the story of fellow prospectors "Lying George" Carmack, Skookum Jim and Tagish Charley, and how word of their gold discovery put the name "Klondike" on the lips of millions around the globe.

As with *The Battles of the War of 1812*, Pierre Berton delivers a fast-paced narrative that makes this important event in Canadian history come vividly alive for today's pre-teen and younger teen readers.